BACK FROM NEAR EXTINCTION

GIANT GALÁPAGOS
TORTOISE

by Tammy Gagne

Content Consultant
Danielle Edwards
Assistant Professor, Quantitative and Systems Biology
University of California, Merced

Core Library

An Imprint of Abdo Publishing
abdopublishing.com

abdopublishing.com

Published by Abdo Publishing, a division of ABDO, PO Box 398166, Minneapolis, Minnesota 55439. Copyright © 2017 by Abdo Consulting Group, Inc. International copyrights reserved in all countries. No part of this book may be reproduced in any form without written permission from the publisher. Core Library™ is a trademark and logo of Abdo Publishing.

Printed in the United States of America, North Mankato, Minnesota
092016
012017

**THIS BOOK CONTAINS
RECYCLED MATERIALS**

Cover Photo: Nick Dale/iStockphoto
Interior Photos: Nick Dale/iStockphoto, 1; David Hosking/Science Source, 4; Bettmann/Getty Images, 8; Shutterstock Images, 10; Frans Lanting/MINT Images/Science Source, 12, 22, 45; John Beatty/Science Source, 15, 27, 43; Ralph Lee Hopkins/Science Source, 16; Encyclopaedia Britannica/UIG/Getty Images, 19; Wolfgang Kaehler/LightRocket/Getty Images, 28; Dolores Ochoa/AP Images, 32, 37; George Holton/Science Source, 38

Editor: Megan Anderson
Series Designer: Jake Nordby

Publisher's Cataloging-in-Publication Data

Names: Gagne, Tammy, author.
Title: Giant Galápagos tortoise / by Tammy Gagne.
Description: Minneapolis, MN : Abdo Publishing, 2017. | Series: Back from near
    extinction | Includes bibliographical references and index.
Identifiers: LCCN 2016945426 | ISBN 9781680784664 (lib. bdg.) |
    ISBN 9781680798517 (ebook)
Subjects: LCSH: Galápagos tortoise --Juvenile literature.
Classification: DDC 597.92--dc23
LC record available at http://lccn.loc.gov/2016945426

CONTENTS

BACK AGAIN

The sun had risen long ago on Isabela Island. But the Galápagos tortoise had only been awake a short while. The giant reptile took its time moving from the warm mud where it slept. It was on its way to munch on a hanging vine.

The tortoise noticed a small ground finch nearby. The tiny bird started rubbing the tortoise's front leg with its beak. The tortoise stretched out its neck.

Wild Galápagos tortoises live exclusively on the Galápagos Islands.

But it had no plans to harm the finch.

The finch had seen a tick crawling up the tortoise's leg. Before the giant creature took another step, the bird gobbled up the pest. The finch had done the tortoise a favor by removing the tick. And it had found its own breakfast in the process.

The finch distracted the tortoise from munching on the vine. Instead, the tortoise remained still under the morning sun. There was no need for the tortoise to rush. There was always grass nearby.

Lucky to Be Alive

Tortoises have roamed the Galápagos Islands for centuries. These islands form an archipelago off the coast of Ecuador. The Galápagos tortoise caught the eye of English naturalist Charles Darwin. Darwin visited the Galápagos Islands in 1835. The tortoise is believed to have played a big role in the development of Darwin's theory of evolution.

Over time, 14 species have evolved from the original Galápagos tortoises. This is a process called adaptive radiation. Some species are specific to a single island. But some islands have more than one species. These species are part of the same genus, *Chelonoidis*. A genus is a category that contains species with similar characteristics.

Approximately 250,000 of these reptiles lived on the Galápagos Islands during the 1600s. Over time, both people and other animals threatened the

Darwin's studies of the tortoises and the islands' other species played a key role in his work on evolution.

tortoises. By the 1970s, only approximately 3,000 of them remained.

Some of the largest threats to Galápagos tortoises were whalers, fur sealers, and pirates. Starting in the 1600s, these people quickly learned that the tortoises were a handy source of food.

The animals could go long periods without eating or drinking. Sailors could put the tortoises on their ships and kill them when they needed food.

Other threats harmed the tortoises too. Visitors brought other animals to the islands. Both goats and rats caused major problems for the Galápagos tortoise. Goats competed with tortoises for native plants. This threatened the tortoises' food source. Rats ate tortoise hatchlings, threatening the population.

Darwin's Discoveries

When he visited the Galápagos Islands, Darwin noticed differences in the shells of these large reptiles. Saddleback tortoises have shells that rise in the front like saddles. This feature allows them to extend their necks higher. This helps them eat tall plants. Dome-shaped tortoises do not have this feature. Since these tortoises eat food off the ground, they do not need the rising shells. The more Darwin studied the tortoises, the better he understood how they had adapted to their environments.

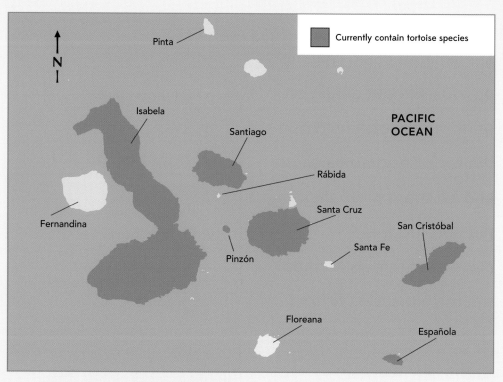

The Galápagos Islands

Galápagos tortoises currently exist on many of the Galápagos Islands. How might being separated by water have caused the tortoises to evolve into distinct species? How might conditions on an island affect the way tortoises live there?

By the 1960s the Galápagos tortoise was endangered. Conservationists started trying to save the species in the 1970s. They used captive breeding to increase the tortoise population. Tortoises were kept at the Charles Darwin Research Station in Ecuador. The tortoises reproduced in a controlled environment. Later they were returned to their homes. Researchers also worked to remove rats and goats from the islands.

More than 40 years later, studies have shown how successful these efforts were. After almost becoming extinct, tortoises are now thriving on the Galápagos Islands.

EXPLORE ONLINE

Chapter One discusses some of Darwin's observations about the Galápagos tortoise during his visit to the islands. As you know, every source is different. How is the information given in the website below different from the information in this chapter? What information is the same? What can you learn from this website?

American Museum of Natural History: Galápagos Tortoises and Evolution

mycorelibrary.com/giant-galapagos-tortoise

CHAPTER TWO

A LARGE AND LONG–LIVED TORTOISE

The first thing most people notice about the Galápagos tortoise is its massive size. It is the largest tortoise in the world. Galápagos tortoises can weigh up to 550 pounds (250 kg). They can measure up to 5 feet (1.5 m) long.

Carrying around all that weight is hard work. So Galápagos tortoises have strong, thick legs. But they don't spend much time on their feet. The tortoises

Sturdy legs support the Galápagos tortoise's large body and protective shell.

prefer lying down and resting as much as possible. They are usually found eating, relaxing in the sun, and cooling off in mud puddles.

The Galápagos tortoise moves from one side to the other as it walks. It never walks in a straight line. That is because the tortoise's front legs turn inward. But most of the time the tortoise doesn't walk at all. The animal pushes with its back legs, forcing the front ones to slide forward.

Baby Tortoises

In 1970 there were only 19 tortoises on Pinzón Island. These tortoises were an average of 70 years old. Because rats were eating so many tortoise eggs, scientists worried the species might go extinct from the island. Some thought no tortoise eggs had hatched on the island of Pinzón in 150 years. In December 2014, however, a research team discovered ten baby Galápagos tortoises on the island.

The Tortoise's Habitat

The tortoise's only natural habitat is the Galápagos Islands. The word *galápagos* means "tortoise" in

The Galápagos Islands provide an ideal habitat for the tortoises.

Spanish. Spanish settlers named the islands after the tortoise.

The islands are located in the tropics, a region near the equator. The region typically has higher temperatures than places farther north or south. Because of their tropical setting, the Galápagos

Tortoises feed on low-lying plants they can reach from the ground.

Islands offer the animals plenty of food, sunshine, and warm air. Reptiles cannot make their own body heat. They depend on their habitat's climate to keep them warm.

Not all of the islands are the same. Some are hot and dry. Tortoises on these islands stay warm easily both day and night. Other islands are somewhat cooler and wetter. A tortoise on one of these islands may lie in the sun during the day. At night it might move into mud, water, or brush to stay warm.

Diet and Mating

The Galápagos tortoise is an herbivore. It eats a variety of plants and grasses. One of the foods it eats the most is the pear cactus. The tortoise also eats other fruits, flowers, and leaves. All of these things are easy for the Galápagos tortoise to bite and chew. The tortoise has no teeth. It must bite its food with the edge of its mouth. It then mashes up this food with the edge of its mouth and swallows it quickly.

The Galápagos tortoise can go up to a year without food. It can also go up to a year without water. When it does eat and drink, it can consume large amounts. Some tortoises eat 77 pounds (35 kg) of food in just one day. A Galápagos tortoise has a bladder at the back of its neck. That is where it stores the water it drinks. The animal's body uses the water as needed.

The Galápagos tortoise becomes an adult at between 20 and 25 years of age. This is when the animals start looking for mates and reproducing. A male will bellow and bob its head up and down to attract a female.

After mating, female tortoises travel several miles to hatching grounds. They look for a dry, sandy place to lay their eggs. Tortoises typically dig a hole 12 inches (30 cm) deep, lay the eggs, and cover them with sand. A Galápagos tortoise egg is the size of a tennis ball.

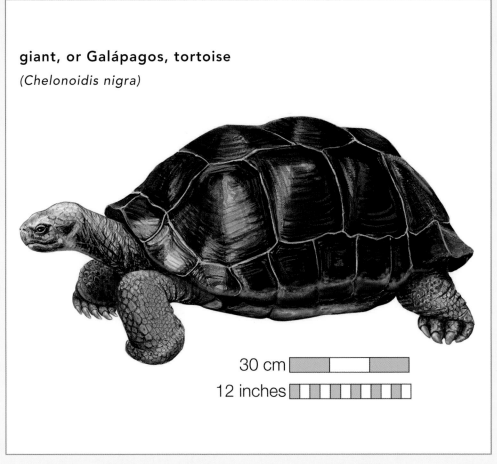

giant, or Galápagos, tortoise
(Chelonoidis nigra)

30 cm

12 inches

Galápagos Tortoise Anatomy

Take a look at this illustration of a Galápagos tortoise. What features of the tortoise's anatomy do you recognize from what you read in the text? How do these features help the tortoise survive in its habitat? How might these features help or hurt the tortoise if it were moved to a different habitat?

An Easygoing Species

In some ways the Galápagos tortoise's laid-back

lifestyle helped decrease the species' numbers.

Fishermen brought goats to the islands in 1959. Goats began eating the same grasses and plants as the tortoises. The peaceful tortoises did not defend their territory. The goats began reproducing. There were more than 40,000 by the 1970s. In 1997 the goat population hit 100,000.

Rats also hurt the Galápagos tortoise population. The rats wanted the tortoises' eggs. The rats killed the reptiles' offspring, sometimes before they could hatch.

Goats and rats had a dramatic impact on the tortoises. The reptiles' long life span was the

Lonesome George

In 2012 a famous Galápagos tortoise known as Lonesome George died. Scientists think he was about 100 years old at the time. George was the last known member of the Pinta Island species. This species was thought to be extinct until George was discovered in 1971. At that time, conservationists got involved. They tried to help George reproduce. But the tortoise showed no interest in mating. After four decades the project had failed to produce a single baby tortoise.

only thing working in their favor. A Galápagos tortoise can live 100 years or longer. It is one of the oldest living animals in the world. But for the species to survive, the tortoises needed to live long enough to reproduce.

FURTHER EVIDENCE

This chapter offers information about the Galápagos tortoise's appearance and behavior. What do you think is the main point of the chapter? What evidence was given to support that point? Visit the website below to learn more about how large this giant tortoise species can grow. Choose a quote from the website that relates to this chapter. Does this quote support the author's main point? Does it make a new point? Write a few sentences explaining how the quote you found relates to this chapter.

Guinness World Records—Largest Tortoise
mycorelibrary.com/giant-galapagos-tortoise

CHAPTER THREE

TORTOISE THREATS

The Galápagos tortoise lives in a beautiful and peaceful setting. The warm islands are filled with lush green plants and white sandy beaches. The scenery and wildlife attract many tourists. All this attention has hurt the Galápagos tortoise.

In the 1960s only about 1,000 tourists came to the Galápagos Islands each year. Now approximately

The arrival of large numbers of tourists on the islands represents one threat to the Galápagos tortoise.

Could Cloning Save Tortoise Species?

Some people wonder why scientists haven't considered cloning to save some species of Galápagos tortoises. Cloning is when an animal is grown from the cells of another. This process would create a new identical tortoise. But cloning actually isn't an option for the tortoise. While scientists can clone many mammals, they are still learning how the process would work with reptiles. Cloning also wouldn't help if a tortoise species had only male or only female tortoises remaining. That's because a cloned reptile would not be able to produce another member of the species. Scientists would need another full-blooded male or female.

170,000 people travel to the Galápagos every year. These visitors bring pollution and trash to the islands from their boats and planes.

Many people have also moved from the mainland of Ecuador to the islands over the centuries. Some of them were looking for work on the islands. In 1990 the population of the Galápagos Islands was 9,735. Today the islands are home to more than 40,000 people. And the number is increasing steadily. The increased population has taken over land, food, and other natural resources from the animals.

Nonnative Species

One of the biggest threats to the Galápagos tortoise has been nonnative species. As people came to the islands over the centuries, they brought other animals with them. In addition to goats and rats, they brought cattle and dogs. These foreign species have had a devastating effect on the native tortoises.

Like the rats brought to the islands by sailors, wild dogs threatened tortoise eggs and young tortoises. It is now illegal to own a pet dog in the Galápagos Islands. That is because these animals pose threats to the native wildlife. But previous visitors brought dogs to the islands. Some of them ran away from their owners. Others were set loose. Stray dogs soon began breeding. This resulted in a large population of homeless dogs that threaten the Galápagos tortoise. Even though they are banned, dogs are often seen in many places on the islands.

People also brought cattle to the islands over the years. Like goats, these animals eat many of the same plants as the Galápagos tortoise. This has had a negative effect on tortoise populations.

Climate Change

Climate change has also affected the tortoises. Climate change is the warming of Earth's atmosphere over time as a result of human activity. Climate change has increased both temperatures and rainfall in the Galápagos Islands. The hot weather can cause the animals to migrate. Tortoises are forced to move to places with conditions that make it harder for them to lay their eggs.

Wet conditions caused by increased rainfall are especially hard on the species. If the sand becomes too wet, Galápagos tortoise eggs won't hatch. When it rains too much, creeks overflow. This also poses dangers for the tortoises. The animals can be washed away by floodwaters.

Wild goats on the islands have had a severe impact on tortoise populations.

Baby Galápagos tortoises are especially vulnerable to the threats the species faces.

Rainfall results in more plants on the islands. That also increases the number of insects. Some of these bugs make it tougher for tortoises to reproduce. Tortoises use dry, sandy ground as a nesting spot for their eggs. Fire ants invade these areas and destroy eggs before they can hatch. Some even attack baby tortoises.

Poaching and Other Threats

It is illegal to hunt and kill Galápagos tortoises. But some people still kill these animals and sell the meat. Because the meat

Egg Relocation

Conservationists have helped the Galápagos tortoise immensely through captive breeding programs. These programs focus on raising tortoises away from their natural habitat. One such program was started on the island of Pinzón in 1965. These conservationists moved tortoise eggs from the wild into the tortoise center on Pinzón. Moving the tortoise eggs kept predators from eating them. Workers waited until the tortoises were four to five years old before releasing them. At this age, the tortoises are big enough that rats can no longer harm them. Without the help of such breeding programs, the Galápagos tortoise likely would have gone extinct.

is so rare, poachers can sell it for high prices. Rangers in Galápagos National Park usually find the shells of these animals when this happens. Poachers have killed at least 120 Galápagos tortoises since 1990.

In a 2014 interview, biologist Godfrey Merlen was asked about the biggest changes he'd seen in his 40 years of working on the Galápagos Islands:

> *In one word; transport. The explosion of transport systems between the South American continent and the Galápagos Islands has been staggering. There were no scheduled flights when I arrived. . . . Today three companies serve the islands and multiple flights arrive every day. Positive in the sense that you can come and go more or less as you like. Negative in that there is no doubt that the continuing arrival of new species is due to cargo boats and aircraft that transit the seas and air. Many species are not invasive, but it is extremely difficult to know which will be and which not. Some have arrived that are extremely dangerous for the fragile oceanic island ecosystems.*

Source: Matt Kareus. "Forty Years Spent Fighting for the Galápagos: An Interview with Dr. Godfrey Merlen." Natural Habitat Adventures. *Natural Habitat Adventures, August 27, 2014. Web. Accessed August 11, 2016.*

Consider Your Audience

Read Merlen's answer carefully. Write a blog post explaining his answer for a new audience, such as a sibling or classmate. How would you explain the positive and negative parts of increased travel to your new audience? How does your blog post differ from Merlen's original answer?

CHAPTER FOUR

LOOKING AHEAD

Conservationists have worked hard to bring the Galápagos tortoise back from the brink of extinction. Although Charles Darwin died in 1882, his name lives on in the Charles Darwin Foundation (CDF). The CDF and its research station are located on Santa Cruz Island. It employs more than 150 scientists. They work closely with the

Breeding programs are ensuring that the Galápagos tortoise has a bright future.

government of Ecuador to save many animal species, including the Galápagos tortoise.

The CDF was established in 1959. That same year, Galápagos National Park was created. The purpose of a national park is to preserve land, plants, and animals within a region. Since then, the CDF and Galápagos National Park have worked together to save the Galápagos tortoise and many other species. The CDF even advises Ecuador's government on how to manage the park and protect threatened species.

The CDF's biggest accomplishment has been its breeding programs. Approximately 50,000 Galápagos tortoises now live on the islands thanks to efforts to raise tortoises into young adulthood. None of the surviving species are endangered.

Ongoing Work

The Galápagos tortoise is doing remarkably well. But conservationists must work hard to keep tortoise populations up. Protecting the tortoises from invasive species is a big part of this process. One of the most important steps has been fencing off land. This keeps goats and other nonnative animals from eating the tortoises' food supply.

Conservationists have also worked to remove goats from the Galápagos Islands. Starting in 1997, Project Isabela used hunting to get rid of goats on Isabela, Pinta, and Santiago. Pinta became free of goats by 2003. By 2006, there were no goats on Santiago or northern Isabela Island. Now conservationists are focusing on doing the same for the islands of Floreana and Pinzón.

New Species

In late 2015 scientists discovered two new species of the Galápagos tortoise. The two species, which live on the island of Santa Cruz, were thought to be the same. But a closer look at their DNA showed that they are different. Each one is actually more closely related to species on other islands than to each other. People call the tortoises living on the east side of the island Cerro Fatal tortoises. Those living on the west side are known as Reserva tortoises.

The Power of Many

The Galápagos Conservancy, Yale University, the government of Ecuador, and the Houston Zoo have accomplished great things for the Galápagos tortoise. In 2015 they all sent volunteers to the Galápagos Islands as part of the Wolf Expedition. This project took place near Wolf Volcano on Isabela Island. The volunteers collected data and observations about the tortoises and their health.

Rats have proven a bit more difficult to control. But conservationists continue to work to keep these predators away from Galápagos tortoise eggs. The quickest way to kill rats in most places is by using poison. But conservationists needed to kill the rats without harming other animal or plant species in the Galápagos. At first the biggest successes took place on the smaller islands, such as Rábida. Rats were successfully removed from Pinzón in 2012. Covering a volcano on the island with poisoned rat bait has helped reduce these populations.

Young tortoises in breeding programs are raised in captivity before being released into the wild.

Saving the Española Species

One of the most successful Galápagos tortoise conservation programs involved the Española species. Named for the island on which they live, these tortoises were close to extinction in the 1960s. The island is very accessible. That made it easy for whalers to find and catch the animals. For a century, they hunted the tortoises without regard for the

Conservationists measure wild tortoises and study their behavior and movements to learn how to better protect them.

species' numbers. By the 1960s, only 14 Española tortoises remained.

Between 1963 and 1974, scientists removed the tortoises and launched a breeding program on Santa Cruz. Slowly the population of the species started to grow. Scientists learned more about how to successfully breed the tortoises. They were able to improve the program. Eventually they brought more than 1,500 Española tortoises back to the island.

The tortoises began breeding naturally by 1990, and the population has stabilized. The incredible success of the breeding program shows the power of smart and dedicated conservation efforts.

The Galápagos Tortoise's Future

Scientists are hopeful for the future of the Galápagos tortoise. With fewer invasive animals, tortoise populations have increased significantly in recent years. There are as many as 5,000 Galápagos tortoises living on Isabela Island alone. Captive breeding programs have proven to help increase the Galápagos tortoise population. Of the 50,000 members of the species living on the islands today, though, only 6,200 were bred in captivity. The tortoises are reproducing with great success on their own now.

Researchers are now studying how and why the giant tortoises are migrating. They have noticed a pattern in this process. When tortoises move from the dry lowlands to the lush highlands, they eat more invasive plants. Invasive plants actually make up more of the tortoises' diets than native ones. Scientists predict that tortoises will depend on these plants more and more in the future. Many of these invasive plants threaten other native species and habitats, so more research must be done. Conservationists do not want to harm the tortoises by removing their food sources.

Saving a species from extinction is no easy matter. It has taken conservationists decades to reverse the decline of the Galápagos tortoise. They are finally seeing the results of their hard work. The giant reptile that came close to dying out is now flourishing on the Galápagos Islands.

Johannah Barry is the president of the Galápagos Conservancy. She explained how this conservation group is working to keep the Galápagos tortoise from facing endangerment in the future:

> Galápagos still has the power to amaze us. Despite the loss of isolation, committed conservation action has kept the vast majority of this archipelago almost untouched by human activity. And those efforts will continue this year with what we believe will be historic outcomes. . . . Dedicated field scientists joined with the genetics team at Yale University to find and capture tortoises previously identified as "high conservation value" individuals representing both the Pinta and Floreana tortoise species. Once the genetics of these tortoises is determined, they will be placed in a captive breeding program and, in just a few generations, it should be possible to obtain tortoises with 95 percent of their "lost" ancestral genes.
>
> Source: Johannah Barry. "From GC's President: Preserving Galápagos in 2016." Galápagos Conservancy. Galápagos Conservancy, January 4, 2016. Web. Accessed August 11, 2016.

Back It Up

Barry uses evidence to support her point. Write a paragraph describing the point she is making. Then write down two or three pieces of evidence Barry uses to make the point.

SPECIES OVERVIEW

Common Name

- Galápagos tortoise

Scientific Name

- *Chelonoidis nigra*

Average Size

- 5 feet (1.5 m) long
- 550 to 573 pounds (249–260 kg) for males, 250 to 300 pounds (113–136 kg) for females

Color

- Brown to light green

Diet

- Flowers, fruits, grasses, and leaves

Average Life Span

- More than 100 years

Habitat

- Varies from dry lowlands to lush highlands

Threats

- Invasive animal species, encroachment, poaching, and climate change
- Endangered status: vulnerable

STOP AND THINK

Surprise Me

Chapter One shared some interesting information about the Galápagos tortoise species. After reading this book, what two or three facts from the chapter did you find most surprising? Why did you find each fact surprising?

Say What?

Learning about species that have faced endangerment can mean learning a lot of new vocabulary. Find five words in this book that you have never seen or heard before. Use a dictionary to find out what they mean. Then write the meanings in your own words, and use each word in a new sentence.

Tell the Tale

Chapter Three discusses the threat of encroachment to the Galápagos tortoise population. Write 200 words from the point of view of a tortoise that was forced to leave its habitat due to a buildup of trash from tourists. Make sure to set the scene, develop a sequence of events, and include a conclusion.

Dig Deeper

After reading this book, what questions do you still have about Galápagos tortoises? With an adult's help, find a few reliable sources that can answer these questions. Write a paragraph about what you learned.

GLOSSARY

archipelago
a series of islands

bladder
a pouch inside an animal that
stores liquid

captive
in a confined area

conservation
preserving and protecting
something

genetics
the study of genes

herbivore
an animal that survives by
eating plant material

invasive
a plant or animal that is
introduced to an area and
harms native species

migrate
to move from one area to
another

poach
to hunt or kill illegally

species
a group of animals or plants
that share basic traits

LEARN MORE

Books

Hamilton, Sue L. *Reptiles*. Minneapolis, MN: Abdo, 2014.

Henzel, Cynthia Kennedy. *Galápagos Islands*. Minneapolis, MN: Abdo, 2011.

Sullivan, Laura L. *Charles Darwin*. Minneapolis, MN: Abdo, 2016.

Websites

To learn more about Back from Near Extinction, visit **booklinks.abdopublishing.com**. These links are routinely monitored and updated to provide the most current information available.

Visit **mycorelibrary.com** for free additional tools for teachers and students.

INDEX

ABOUT THE AUTHOR

Tammy Gagne has written more than 150 books for adults and children. She resides in northern New England with her husband and son. One of her favorite pastimes is visiting schools to talk to kids about the writing process.